Cambridge **Discovery** Education™

▶ **INTERACTIVE READERS**

Series editor: Bob Hastings

HOW COOL IS COLD!

A2

Nic Harris

CAMBRIDGE
UNIVERSITY PRESS

DISCOVERY
EDUCATION™

CAMBRIDGE UNIVERSITY PRESS
Cambridge, New York, Melbourne, Madrid, Cape Town,
Singapore, São Paulo, Delhi, Mexico City

Cambridge University Press
32 Avenue of the Americas, New York, NY 10013-2473, USA

www.cambridge.org
Information on this title: www.cambridge.org/9781107658035

First published 2014

Printed in Hong Kong, China, by Golden Cup Printing Company Limited

A catalog record for this publication is available from the British Library.

Library of Congress Cataloging-in-Publication Data

Harris, Nicholas, 1956-
  How cool is cold! / Nic Harris.
      pages cm. -- (Cambridge discovery interactive readers)
  ISBN 978-1-107-65803-5 (pbk. : alk. paper)
  1. Cold--Juvenile literature. 2. English language--Textbooks for foreign speakers. 3. Readers
(Elementary) I. Title.

QC278.2.H37 2013
551.5'25--dc23

                                    2013024137

ISBN 978-1-107-65803-5

Additional resources for this publication at www.cambridge.org

Layout services, art direction, book design, and photo research: Q2ABillSMITH GROUP
Editorial services: Hyphen S.A.
Audio production: CityVox, New York
Video production: Q2ABillSMITH GROUP

Contents

Before You Read:
Get Ready!

Do you like cold places? What do you do in cold places to stay warm? Let's take a look at cold places around the world and how people and animals live in them.

Words to Know

Look at the pictures. Then complete the sentences with the correct words.

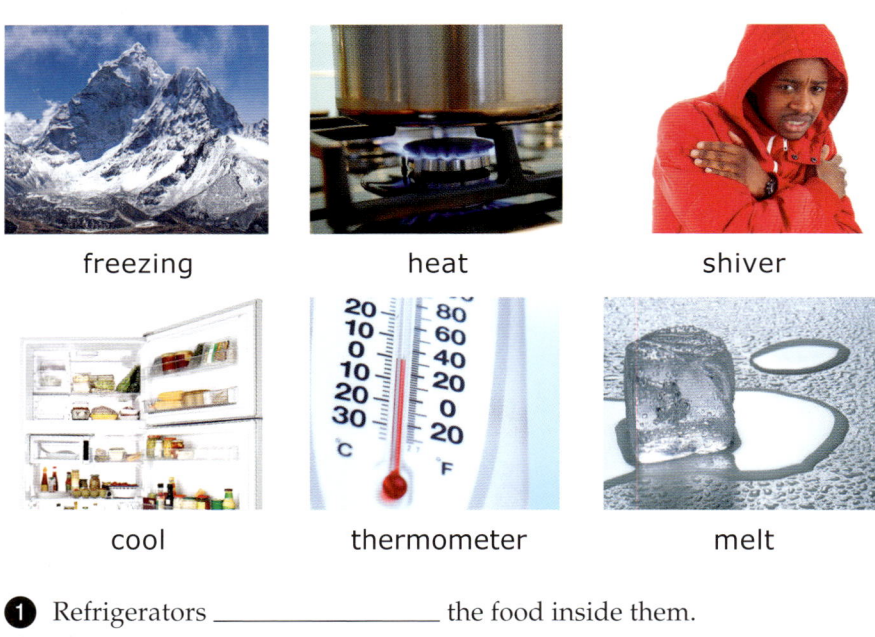

freezing   heat   shiver

cool   thermometer   melt

❶ Refrigerators _____ the food inside them.

❷ The temperature at the top of this mountain is _____.

❸ Today we get the _____ that we need to cook our food from gas or electricity.

❹ A _____ tells us the temperature.

❺ People _____ when they are cold.

❻ When ice gets warm, it starts to _____.

Words to Know

Read the paragraph. Then complete the sentences with the correct highlighted words.

It's good to stay healthy. However, all of us get an illness at some time. We get ill when bad things come into our body and get into our blood. When we have an illness, we feel sick. We also feel weak and tired. Sometimes we get a temperature, and our skin becomes hot. We don't want to go to work or go outside the house!

1. _____ is red, and it travels around the body.
2. When you feel sick, you don't feel strong. You feel _____.
3. _____ is on the outside of the body.
4. An _____ is a problem we have with our health.

CHAPTER 1

It's Too Cold!

TURN ON THE FIRE, PUT ON SOME WARM CLOTHES, AND MAKE YOURSELF A HOT DRINK. THIS BOOK IS GOING TO MAKE YOU FEEL COLD!

The weather for the weekend is going to be very cold. We'll see temperatures as low as −15° C in some places, and there will be a lot of wind and snow. Driving will be dangerous because of ice on the roads. So wear warm clothes and drive carefully.

Weather like this is bad news for many people. **Freezing** weather makes life difficult. Airports close, trains stop running, and walking on sidewalks[1] becomes difficult because of ice.

These problems are bad for everyone living in cold places. But does everyone *feel* the cold in the same way?

[1]**sidewalk:** a place next to a road where people can walk

Studies show that cold weather is worse for older people. Older people don't shiver as quickly or as much as younger people. When you shiver, your body makes **heat** and you get warmer. Thin people feel the cold more than people who are big and heavy. Heavy people have more fat on their bodies. The fat helps their body heat stay inside and keeps them warmer.

The cold can be wonderful or terrible. Think about a cold drink full of ice on a hot day, or a cold shower in a freezing bathroom. In this book we're going to look at cold places, how the cold **affects** our health, people who live in the far north, and animals with "cold blood."

?

APPLY

Think of a time in your life when you felt very cold. Where were you? What were you doing? Did you shiver?

CHAPTER 2

Cold Places

WINTER MAY BE COLD WHERE YOU LIVE. BUT IS IT AS COLD AS IN THESE PLACES?

International Falls, Minnesota, USA, is known as "The Icebox of the Nation." This town of 7,000 people is the coldest town in the country. In January 2011, the **thermometer** showed a temperature of –32° C! The normal temperature in January is –15° C.

The city of Yakutsk, in Russia, is the coldest city in the world. The daily high in January is around –50° C, but it can get as cold as –64° C. And the winters are eight months long. When people get out of their cars here, they do not turn off their **engines**. They keep the engines going so that they don't freeze. Also, people do not wear metal[2] glasses outside. It is so cold that the metal sticks to[3] their skin, and they cannot take them off.

[2] **metal:** something hard and strong that people make things out of
[3] **stick to:** stay on something else

Antarctica is the driest, windiest, and coldest place on Earth. In July 1983, it was –89.2° C. That's the lowest temperature ever recorded[4] on Earth. Very few animals can live in Antarctica, and there are no towns for people, only some science stations. About 20 scientists live at the Vostok Science Station in Antarctica, but they do not live there all year.

Antarctica has 90 percent of the world's ice, and in some places the ice goes down more than 4,700 meters! But there is a problem. Warm sea water that gets under the ice is making it melt. If lots of this ice becomes **liquid**, the seas in the world will get higher. This will mean some towns near the sea will be under the water.

[4] **record:** When you record a piece of information, you write it down.

Antarctica: the coldest place on Earth

So it can be very cold on Earth. But how cold is it on other planets?

It is colder on the planet Mars than it is on Earth. This is because it is usually farther away from the Sun than our world is. The coldest temperature on Mars is –140° C.

There are eight planets in our solar system. As the planets get farther away from the Sun, they usually get colder. But not always. Neptune is the farthest planet from the Sun, but it is not the coldest. Today, that prize goes to Uranus. The temperature on Uranus is –224° C. It is colder than Neptune because the temperature at the center of the planet is colder. Also, it has very strong winds – sometimes more than 800 kilometers an hour!

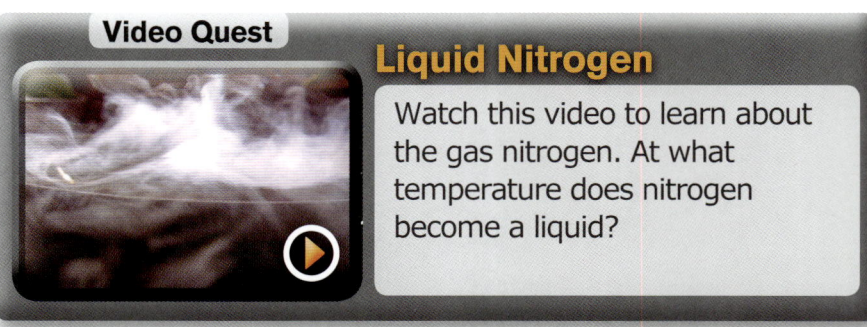

Video Quest

Liquid Nitrogen

Watch this video to learn about the gas nitrogen. At what temperature does nitrogen become a liquid?

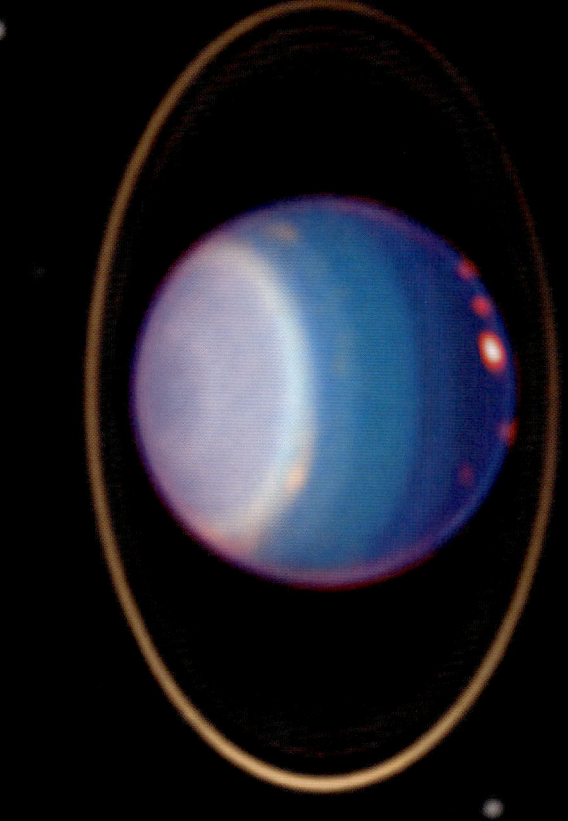

Uranus is the coldest planet.

Scientists say that the coldest temperature is –273.15° C. This is called 0 Kelvin. Nothing can be colder. The normal temperature in space is about –265° C. In 2000, a group of scientists cooled a piece of metal to –273.15° C. On that day, that piece of metal was the coldest thing in the universe![5]

....

[5] **universe:** everything that is around us: air, space, the stars, the planets

This person has the flu and a high temperature.

CHAPTER 3

Health Problems and the Cold

DOES COLD WEATHER MAKE YOU SICK?

Many people think that cold weather makes you sick, but it isn't as simple as that. It is true that in winter more people catch **colds**. This happens when something called a virus comes into the body through the eyes, ears, nose, or mouth. Many doctors think that people get colds in the winter because they spend more time together inside. This makes it easier for the viruses to go from one person to another.

Although a cold isn't a serious[6] illness, the influenza virus, or **flu**, can be. Your body hurts, and your body temperature can go up to 40° C. People can die from the flu.

[6]**serious:** very bad

Cold weather may not give you a cold, but it can kill you. Hypothermia is a serious illness that often affects people who have accidents while climbing mountains or skiing. It also affects people who don't have homes and live on the streets. A healthy person's body temperature is about 37° C. If it falls to 35° C, hypothermia begins. The person feels weak, and they want to sleep. And at just below 35° C, the body can have heart problems and the brain can stop working.

Anna Bagenholm fell under some ice while skiing in Norway in 1999. She was under the ice for 80 minutes before people **reached** her. She had hypothermia with a body temperature of only 13.7° C.

Her heart stopped. But the low temperature slowed her heart rate[7] down. This helped to preserve[8] her heart and brain so she didn't die. She still goes skiing today!

[7] **heart rate:** how fast or slow your heart goes
[8] **preserve:** keep something as it is when things around it change

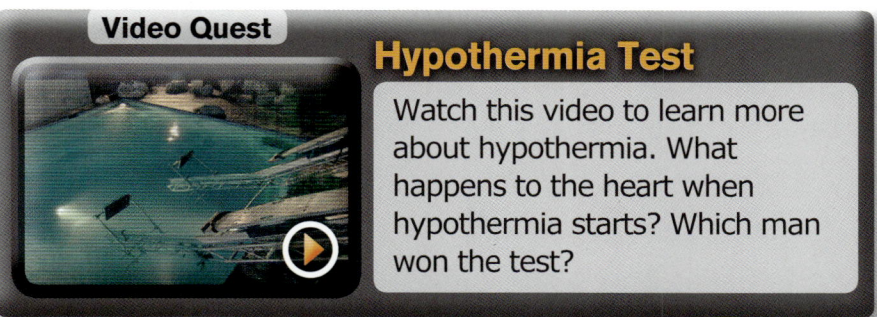

Video Quest

Hypothermia Test

Watch this video to learn more about hypothermia. What happens to the heart when hypothermia starts? Which man won the test?

An Eskimo wearing a parka

CHAPTER 4

The Eskimos

THE ESKIMOS KNOW ALL ABOUT THE COLD. HOW DO THEY STAY WARM AND HEALTHY?

The Eskimos, called Inuits in some places, live in Alaska, Canada, Greenland, and northern Russia. There are about 150,000 in the world today.

Eskimos know how to live with freezing temperatures. Three things are very important when living in cold places: the clothes you wear, the food you eat, and the houses you live in.

Eskimos traditionally[9] make their clothes from animal hair and animal skins. They were the first people to wear a *parka*. A parka is a coat and a hat, called a hood, all in one piece together. Today, Eskimos still wear parkas, but many of them are now made from man-made things, not animal hair and skins.

[9]**traditionally:** in the same way as a long time ago

The traditional Eskimo food is meat from animals such as seals, walruses, and whales. These meats have a lot of fat. Eating foods high in fat helps the Eskimos stay warm. When the body breaks down food, it makes heat. Foods with fat let the body make more heat.

A seal

The Eskimo word *igloo* means "house." These traditional houses are built from ice and hard snow. The Eskimos cut the ice into squares, and they use these

An igloo

to build the igloo. You might think it is cold in an igloo, but it isn't. Eskimos make fires inside the igloo and the snow keeps the heat in.

Today, most Eskimos live in modern houses in villages. But they still build igloos when they travel away from home.

? EVALUATE

How is living in an igloo different from living in a normal house? Would you like to wear Eskimo clothes? Would you like their food?

CHAPTER 5

Cold-blooded Animals

COLD TEMPERATURES AND CHANGING TEMPERATURES AFFECT ANIMALS, TOO. LET'S LOOK AT SOME OF THEM.

The Earth is home to two kinds of animals: warm-blooded and cold-blooded. We are warm-blooded and so are most animals that have hair. Warm-blooded animals make heat inside their bodies and have a temperature of about 37° C. They can normally keep this temperature if the outside temperature is not too cold or too hot. Much of the food they eat makes heat, which they need in cold weather.

A lizard

Snakes are an example of a cold-blooded animal. These animals do not make much heat inside their bodies. The temperature of their blood goes up and down with the temperature around them. If the weather is cold, the snake's blood is also colder. But if the weather is warm and sunny, the snake's blood gets warmer.

When cold-blooded animals feel cold, they like to lie down in the sun. When they feel too hot, they find a place away from the sunlight. Cold-blooded animals do not need to eat as much, or as often, as warm-blooded animals. They don't need to use the food to heat their bodies.

Very cold weather is dangerous for cold-blooded animals, too. When their blood is too cold, they feel weak. It is difficult for them to move around and look for food. Some will go to a warmer place. Others, like snakes and lizards, often sleep for many days in warmer places, for example, under rocks.

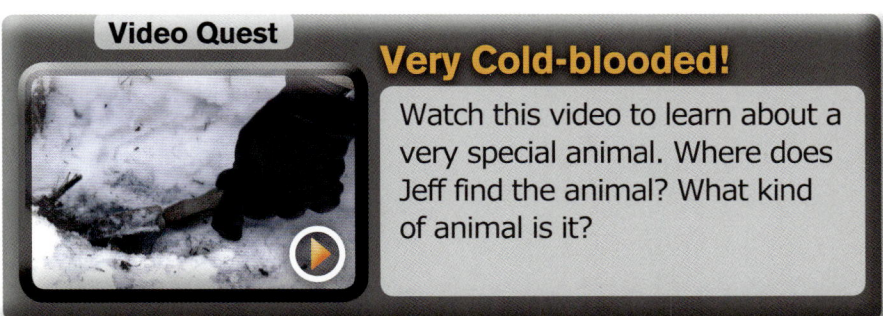

Video Quest

Very Cold-blooded!

Watch this video to learn about a very special animal. Where does Jeff find the animal? What kind of animal is it?

CHAPTER 6

New Ways to Use Cold

SOMETIMES WE USE THE WORD "COLD" TO TALK ABOUT MORE THAN THE WEATHER.

Hal told his dad he wanted to be a singer in a music group, but his dad <u>threw cold water</u> on the idea.

What do you think this expression[10] means? Think about someone suddenly throwing cold water on you. How does that feel? So does Hal's dad like Hal's idea or not?

Anna is very <u>cold hearted</u>. She never listens to her friends' problems.

What about this expression? What does it mean? In very cold weather you sometimes cannot feel things with some parts of your body, for example, the ends of your fingers. So what kind of person is Anna if her heart is cold? Is she a good friend?

[10] **expression:** something people often say

*Lori said she wanted to marry John. Then, she got
<u>cold feet</u>.*

Think of this: You want to go swimming in the
sea. You put your foot in the water and it is very cold.
Do you go farther into the water? Maybe you do, and
maybe you don't. So, is Lori excited to marry John, or is
she worried about it?

*Simon gave Jim <u>the cold shoulder</u>[11] and walked away
without saying hello.*

Normally, people talk to each other face to face. But
this time, Simon turned away. Do you think Simon feels
angry or happy with Jim?

[11]**shoulder:** the part of your body at the top of your arm

> **? ANALYZE**
>
> Think about the expressions in this chapter.
> Now read this one: *The baseball hit David on
> the head very hard. He fell down and was <u>out
> cold</u>.* What do you think it means?

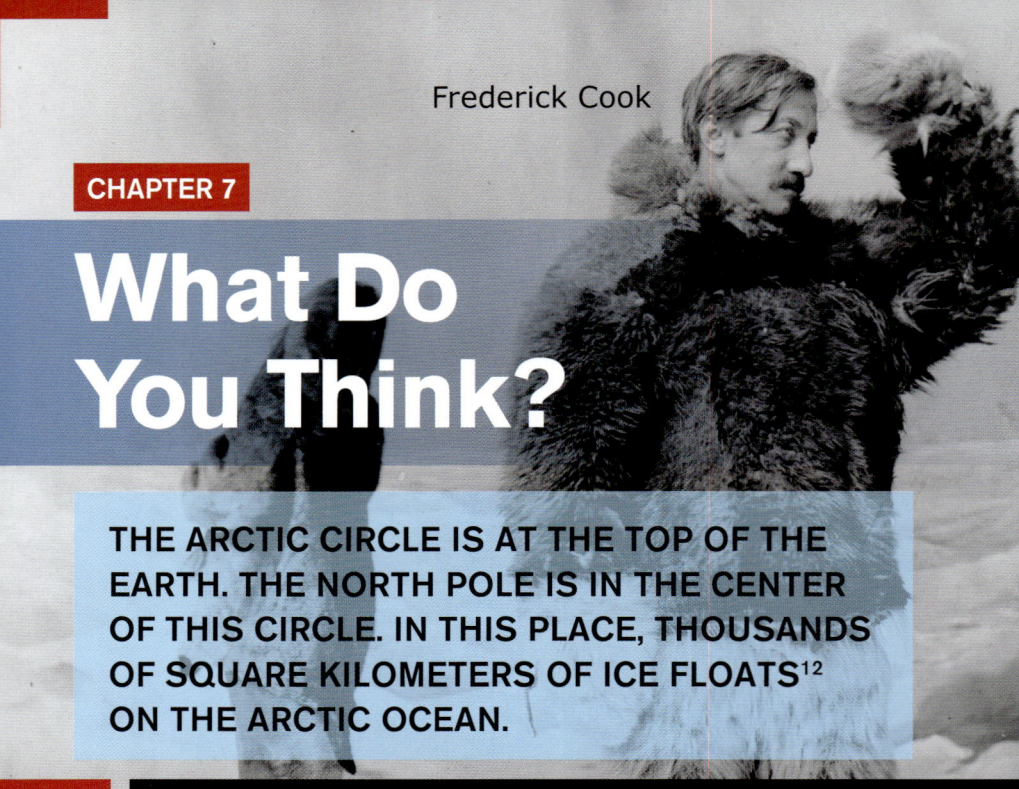

Frederick Cook

CHAPTER 7

What Do You Think?

THE ARCTIC CIRCLE IS AT THE TOP OF THE EARTH. THE NORTH POLE IS IN THE CENTER OF THIS CIRCLE. IN THIS PLACE, THOUSANDS OF SQUARE KILOMETERS OF ICE FLOATS[12] ON THE ARCTIC OCEAN.

Could you reach the top of the Earth on foot? For several hundred years, many explorers[13] tried to do just that. Some died in freezing weather, but others got there.

In 1909, American Frederick Cook claimed[14] that he reached the North Pole. Then, a week later, another American, Robert Peary, claimed that he was the first to reach the North Pole. So who reached it? And if they both did, who reached it first?

[12] **float:** stay on top of water
[13] **explorer:** someone who travels to places where no one has ever been to find out what is there
[14] **claim:** say that something is true or is a fact

In 2011, the National Geographic Society studied information that Peary kept from his trip. They said it showed that Peary reached the North Pole. But nobody could prove[15] that Cook also got there. Other people, however, have studied different information, and they think that Cook reached the Pole and Peary didn't! We may never know for sure. Both men said they left notes at the pole, but no one has ever found either note.

Robert Peary

But we do know that in 1968, American Ralph Plaisted was the first man (without question) to reach the North Pole by land. He and others in his group reached it by snowmobile.

How would you like to travel to the North Pole? Think about your answers to these questions:

- You have to take a friend. Which of your friends do you choose and why?

- What food will you take? Remember it can't be too heavy.

You will need to take important things like warm clothes with you. But what other things will you take?

---

[15] **prove:** show a particular result after a period of time

After You Read

Read the following sentences and choose Ⓐ, Ⓑ, or Ⓒ.

1 People in the Vostok Science Station in Antarctica _____.

   Ⓐ live there all year

   Ⓑ live in a science station

   Ⓒ live outside in igloos

2 The planet Mars is colder than the Earth because _____.

   Ⓐ it's smaller than the Earth

   Ⓑ it moves faster than the Earth

   Ⓒ it's farther from the Sun

3 If you have the flu, your body temperature _____.

   Ⓐ goes up

   Ⓑ stays the same

   Ⓒ goes down to 35° C

4 A parka is something an Eskimo _____.

   Ⓐ eats

   Ⓑ wears

   Ⓒ rides in

5 The temperature of a snake's blood _____.

   Ⓐ changes all the time

   Ⓑ stays the same all the time

   Ⓒ gets hotter in winter

6 To have *cold feet* means _____.

   Ⓐ you do not listen to your friends

   Ⓑ you don't want to do something

   Ⓒ you do not like something

7 In 1909 Peary and Cook _____.

   Ⓐ tried to get to the North Pole but didn't arrive there

   Ⓑ both claimed they were the first person to reach the North Pole

   Ⓒ traveled together to the North Pole

Complete the Text

Use the words in the box to complete the paragraph below.

| blood | cools | heats | illness | shiver | thermometer |

For people, normal **1** _____ temperature is 37° C. Animals have different temperatures, especially snakes and lizards. In freezing weather, our bodies **2** _____ to try to stay warm. We get very sick when our body **3** _____ down to below 35° C. We also feel unwell when our temperature **4** _____ up to 40° C. When we feel sick, we can check our temperature with a **5** _____. If we have a serious **6** _____, like the flu, we might have to see a doctor.

Agree or Disagree?

Read the sentences and decide if you agree or disagree. Then say why.

	AGREE OR DISAGREE?	WHY?
I like the weather in my country.		
I would prefer to live in a cold place rather than a hot place.		
It is easier to live in very cold weather than very hot weather.		

Answer Key

Words to Know, page 4

1 cool **2** freezing **3** heat **4** thermometer **5** shiver
6 melt

Words to Know, page 5

1 Blood **2** weak **3** Skin **4** illness

Apply, page 7
Answers will vary.

Video Quest, page 10
Nitrogen gas changes to a liquid at −300° C.

Video Quest, page 13
With hypothermia the heart rate gets slower, or reduces.
Jonathan wins the test.

Evaluate, page 15
Answers will vary.

Video Quest, page 17
Jeff finds the animal under the snow. The animal is a frog.

Analyze, page 19
To be *out cold* means you are sleeping because something
hit your head.

Choose the Correct Answers, page 22
1 B **2** C **3** A **4** B **5** A **6** B **7** B

Complete the Text, page 23
1 blood **2** shiver **3** cools **4** heats **5** thermometer
6 illness

Agree or Disagree?, page 23
Answers will vary.